ADULT CURSE WORD COLORING BOOK

BOOK 2

JASON POTASH

THIS BOOK BELONGS TO

Yap Kee Chong
8345 NW 66 ST #B7885
Miami, FL 33166

Createspace

Whipped

weeze bag

vajj

jealous

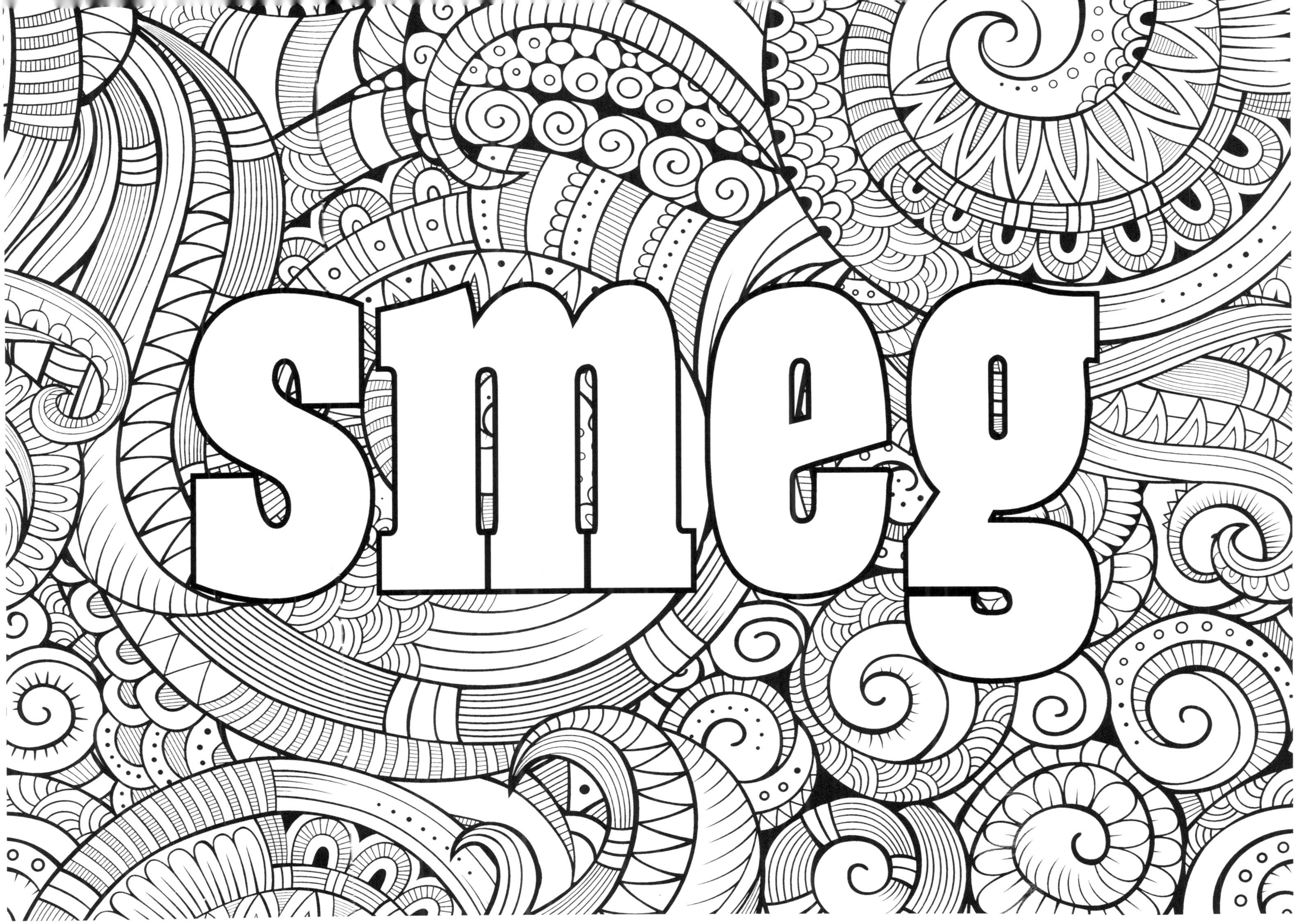
smeg

ruffian

prick

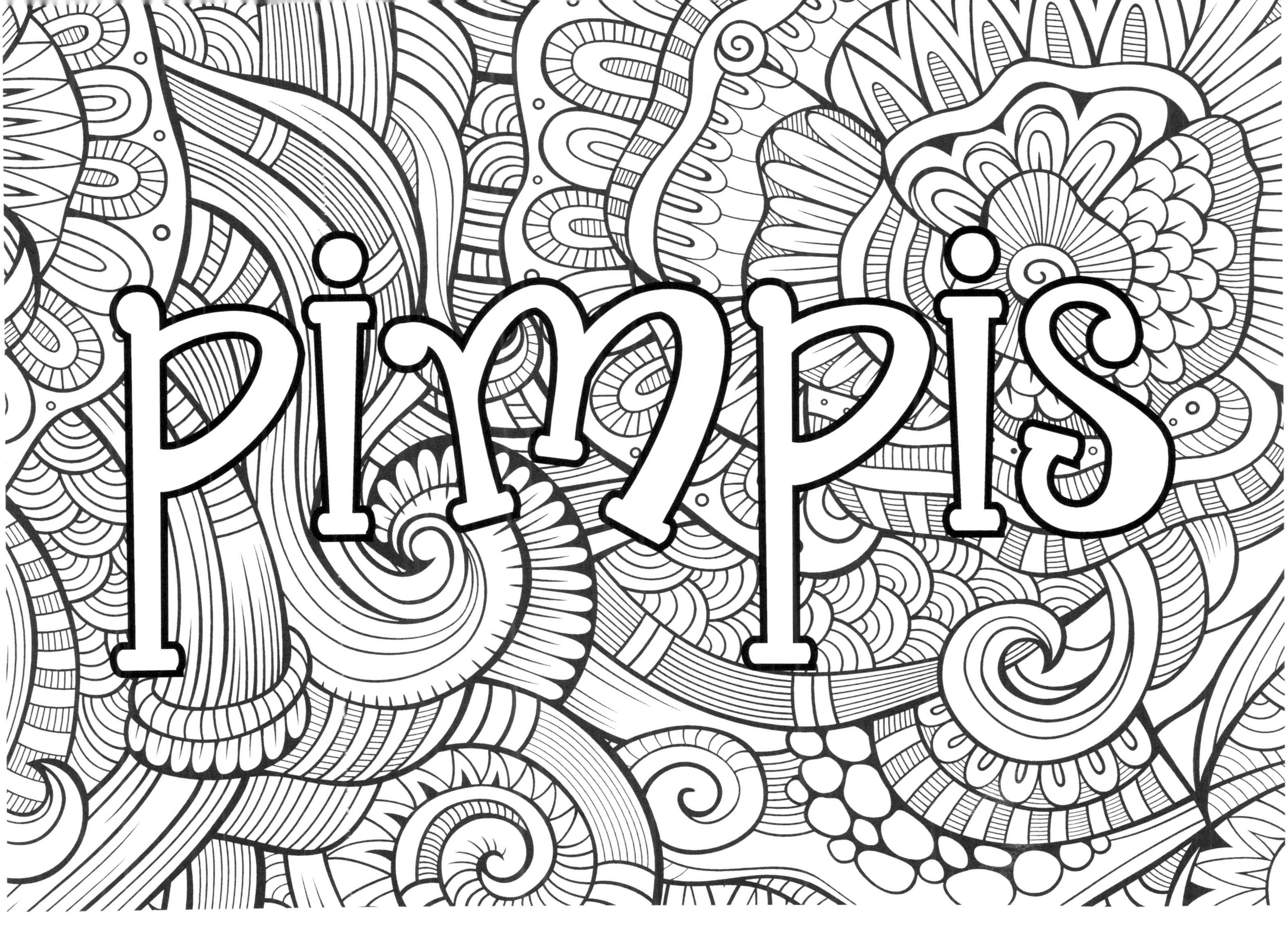
pimpis

phuk

Keep

ZZZ!

idiot

gooch

fuckup

fuck off

fellatio

fanny fuck

dogging

dick
beaters

cumdumpster

cockwaffle

bitching

bastard

assshit

anus

97778018R00033

Made in the USA
Lexington, KY
01 September 2018